How Do Smartphones Affect Health?

By Tammy Gagne

ReferencePoint
Press®

San Diego, CA

LIBRARY OF CONGRESS CATALOGING-IN-PUBLICATION DATA

Name: Gagne, Tammy– author.
Title: How Do Smartphones Affect Health?/by Tammy Gagne.
Description: San Diego, CA: ReferencePoint Press, Inc., [2021] | Series: Smartphones and Society | Audience: Grade 9 to 12 | Includes bibliographical references and index.
ISBN: 978-1-68282-943-1 (hardback)
ISBN: 978-1-68282-944-8 (eBook)
The complete Library of Congress record is available at www.loc.gov.

CONTENTS

SMARTPHONES AND INJURIES

In 2018, *New York Times* reporter Nellie Bowles began experiencing a problem with her right thumb. Her thumb became numb, and it also ached. The pain extended up her arm. She lost the ability to use her right thumb. She consulted with Dr. Sanjeev Kakar, a surgeon who specializes in treating issues with the hand, wrist, and forearm. Kakar got to the root of the issue. Bowles was spending so much time on her smartphone that she was suffering from an injury called De Quervain's tendinosis. This condition is caused by overusing the tendons on the thumb side of the wrist. Kakar had seen an increase in this type of injury related to smartphone addiction. He told Bowles that if she did not change her behavior, she would need surgery to fix the problem. He instructed her to stop typing with her right hand on her smartphone for a while.

Overuse of many digital devices, including smartphones and laptops, can cause hand or wrist pain. This pain comes from a repetitive motion such as texting.

"That sounds logical and easy," Bowles wrote in a 2018 *New York Times* article about her experience, "until you try to email left-handed."[1]

Bowles sought help from acupuncture, which Kakar recommended to help reverse the problem. This ancient

Chinese healing technique involves a trained caregiver inserting tiny needles into the body at points that correspond with specific ailments. Meanwhile, Bowles also scaled back on her smartphone use. Her injury healed, and she was able to avoid the surgery.

SMARTPHONE DEPENDENCE

Few things in modern culture have become as pervasive as the smartphone. These handheld devices allow users to make calls, send and receive emails, browse the internet, and use various types of apps. Smartphones have become enormously popular since they first hit the mainstream market in 2007. Like Bowles, many smartphone users now spend several hours each day on their devices. They have a hard time being away from their smartphones for an extended period of time. This dependence has led many people to suffer from injuries or other health problems. Kakar says, "Kids twenty years ago were not using handheld devices, and now they're using them all the time in schools and at home. We may be at the tip of an iceberg, and we're going to see a cumulative effect."[2]

Warning signs of smartphones' potential negative effects began emerging shortly after their introduction to the masses. Many smartphone users dismissed these early concerns, insisting that people were imagining a problem where there wasn't one, but the health issues persisted. In 2009, writer Dan Childs reported on the potential negative effects of cell phone use for ABC News. He cautioned, "When it comes to the possible downsides of mobile device use, the side effects are not all in

> "Kids twenty years ago were not using handheld devices, and now they're using them all the time in schools and at home. We may be at the tip of an iceberg, and we're going to see a cumulative effect."[2]
>
> *—Dr. Sanjeev Kakar, surgeon at the Mayo Clinic*

People who are addicted to smartphones may also be addicted to other digital devices. These devices can include tablets and laptops.

our heads. Our thumbs, it turns out, may also bear the brunt of our reliance on these devices."[3] Still, more and more people purchased smartphones in the years that followed.

In 2011, 35 percent of Americans owned a smartphone. By 2017, that percentage had more than doubled.

Today, people continue to experience physical and mental health issues when they overuse their smartphones. Many smartphone users complain of injuries in their fingers, thumbs, necks, shoulders, and elbows. These are repetitive motion injuries, or injuries caused by performing the same motion over and over. Other users experience eyestrain or sleeplessness from staring at smartphone screens for too long. Many experts also link mental health issues such as anxiety and depression to too much smartphone use. In 2019, the National Education Association said that anxiety linked to too much smartphone use among students had become a "mental-health tsunami."[4] Like a tsunami wave that causes destruction, smartphones are becoming a disaster of sorts to the people who overuse them. People who spend too much time on these devices often suffer from a myriad of health problems.

WHAT IS THE LINK BETWEEN HEALTH AND SMARTPHONES?

Smartphones have had a profound impact on modern society. Since they were introduced in the first decade of the twenty-first century, these devices have become commonplace. Many smartphone users carry their phones with them all the time. Virtually everywhere smartphone users go, they can call, text, send and receive email, take photos and videos, browse the web, and check their social media accounts. Using the Global Positioning System (GPS), smartphones can tell users where they are and give them directions. Other useful smartphone features include music and video streaming, news and weather updates, and apps for reading, education, and productivity. The list of things that smartphones can do seems endless—and

A typical smartphone owner spends about two hours using apps per day. On average, each person uses about thirty to forty apps per month.

so does the amount of time people are spending on these devices.

Although smartphones have made many aspects of life easier, smartphone overuse has been linked to many physical, mental, and emotional health issues. Dr. Renee Enriquez is a rehabilitation specialist at the University of Texas Southwestern Medical Center in Dallas, Texas.

She helps people cope with illnesses and injuries. In a 2019 interview with *Healthline*, Enriquez said that many people are unaware of the physical injuries that can result from smartphone overuse. She explained, "Selfie elbow, texting thumb, text neck, and 'Nintenditus' are colloquialisms that describe overuse musculoskeletal injuries associated with increased use of modern technology, including but not limited to smartphones, tablets, and video games."[5] The term "Nintenditus" refers to the popular Nintendo video gaming system, but this type of injury can result from playing too many games on any device, including a smartphone.

Thumb injuries are among the most common repetitive motion injuries that arise from smartphone overuse. Over time, continual scrolling, swiping, and texting irritate the tendon in the thumb as it rubs against the tunnel that surrounds it. The inflammation that results from this repeated contact typically causes pain near the knuckle. Some people even report that their thumbs click when they bend them.

Hunching forward to look at a smartphone screen can also cause pain or injury. Maintaining good posture while using the device can prevent nerve pain in the neck, shoulders, and back. Experts recommend keeping a smartphone at eye level during use. Taking regular breaks is also a wise move. Checking the device only once every few hours is ideal, but many people find it challenging to put their smartphones down for that long.

DEADLY DISTRACTIONS

Sometimes the risk involved with using a smartphone isn't about the amount of time the user spends on the device but rather the other things the person tries to do simultaneously. Some people get into car accidents when they try to text or talk on a cell phone while driving. To reduce the number of these accidents, many US states have enacted laws that forbid drivers from using phones. Despite these laws, distracted driving accidents are still common. According to the National Safety Council, texting and driving causes 1.6 million auto crashes in the United States each year. Of all the motor vehicle crash fatalities that occur in the nation, approximately 25 percent are caused by distracted driving.

Smartphones can also be distracting for pedestrians. Injuries that result from walking while using a smartphone have become alarmingly common. Looking down at a phone while walking can be especially dangerous when people do so in or near a roadway. For this reason, several US cities and towns have banned texting while walking.

Rebecca Lindland is an auto analyst. She studies trends in the automobile industry. In a 2018 interview with *USA Today*, she explained,

> *We've got distracted drivers and we've got distracted pedestrians, and that is a deadly combination. At some point in time, people both behind the wheel and walking in the street have to take responsibility for their behavior and put down the phone.*[6]

EYE DAMAGE

Looking at smartphones or other electronic devices for long periods of time can make a person's eyes feel tired and strained. The light given off by the screens causes these issues. To the human eye, the light from a screen looks white, but much of the light is blue. Too much of this blue light can damage the photoreceptors in the eye's retina. Photoreceptors are special cells that react to light. The retina is the part of the eye that is responsible for sight. When light enters the eye, photoreceptors respond by sending images to the brain.

EXPOSURE TO GERMS

One health hazard smartphones pose to users affects them whether they spend hours at a time on their phones or they only use their devices for a short time each day. Researchers at the University of Arizona found that smartphones contain ten times more bacteria than toilet seats. Germs commonly found on the devices include *Streptococcus* and *E. coli*. These are dangerous bacteria that have the potential to make users very ill. The best way to get rid of these germs is to clean a smartphone regularly. This does not mean merely wiping the screen with a dry cloth, but rather cleaning the entire surface of the device using a cloth dipped in a solution of 60 percent water and 40 percent rubbing alcohol. Performing this simple task a few times each month will help protect users from these germs.

Research shows that staring at blue light too long can cause macular degeneration, a disease that can lead to blindness later in life. Dr. Mark Fromer is an ophthalmologist at Lenox Hill Hospital in New York City. He treats people who have eye diseases or disorders. In 2018, he tweeted, "Blue light appears to damage retinal cells. It is still unclear how much blue light and for how long it's necessary to damage these sight-seeing cells. We do know the damage is irreversible."[7]

SLEEP DISRUPTION

During evening hours, looking at too much blue light can throw off a person's circadian rhythm. This is the body's natural tendency to feel more alert during daylight hours and drowsier at night when it gets dark outside. Blue light suppresses the brain's release of melatonin, the hormone that triggers sleepiness. People who spend a lot of time looking at smartphones after dark may have a hard time falling asleep. As a result, they may feel tired during the day. If someone must use a smartphone for an extended period at night, it is wise to reduce the blue light the screen gives off, making it easier on the eyes. Many smartphones offer this option in their settings features. Users who do not like the color change that comes with this setting can opt to use an anti-blue light screen protector instead. Some people even use special eyeglasses that block blue light.

It appears that there are some benefits to looking at a small amount of blue light during the day, however. For example, studies have shown that blue light boosts alertness and can make people feel happier. Some experts say it can even help prevent nearsightedness, a condition that makes it difficult for people to see objects that are far away. But people need to be careful not to overexpose themselves to blue light. "It's really important to know when you're on digital devices all day long, to take breaks every twenty minutes to look away at something that's not digital," advises ophthalmologist Melissa Barnett.[8]

INTERFERENCE WITH HEART DEVICES

Cell phones emit a type of energy called radio frequency (RF) waves. Scientists have confirmed that RF waves pose a serious risk to people who have certain kinds of implanted pacemakers. Some people who have heart problems have these medical devices. A pacemaker sends electrical pulses to the heart to help control a person's heart rate. RF waves cause a problem called electromagnetic interference (EMI). EMI occurs when the RF waves cause a pacemaker to stop working, to deliver pulses irregularly, or to deliver pulses at fixed rates while ignoring the heart's own rhythm. Although the risk for most people who have these devices is low, there is enough cause for concern that the Food and Drug Administration (FDA) recommends that anyone with a pacemaker take certain precautions. These precautions include never carrying a phone close to the medical device and always listening to the phone with the ear on the opposite side of the body from the pacemaker.

Another medical device that can help people who have heart problems is an implantable cardioverter defibrillator (ICD). ICDs deliver small electric shocks to a person's heart in order to stabilize erratic beats. They can restart a person's heart if it stops beating. ICDs can also detect when a person's heart rate is dangerously slow. Then they stimulate the heart to beat faster. Results from a study on ICDs revealed that smartphones can pose a hazard to people who have these medical devices. Researchers at the German Heart Care Center in Munich, Germany, did this study. Although the risk was likewise low for people who had ICDs, it was enough to indicate that the FDA guidelines for pacemakers should also be applied to these medical devices. Health care writer Jeff Minerd reported, "One patient's ICD detected and misinterpreted electromagnetic waves from the Nokia and HTC smartphones as intracardiac signals."[9] This means that the ICD responded to the RF waves as if they were signals coming from the person's heart. As a result, the ICD decreased the person's heart rate.

MENTAL AND EMOTIONAL EFFECTS

The mental and emotional effects of overusing smartphones can be just as serious as the physical effects. According to Apple, the manufacturer of one of the most popular smartphones on the market, the average person unlocks his or her smartphone eighty times each day. Sometimes people use their phones for important tasks such as responding to work emails or letting family members know when they are running late. More often, though, much of a user's time on the device is spent scrolling through social media apps. Many people who spend a lot of time on social media experience feelings of anxiety, depression, and isolation. Even worse, many people feel unable to stop this vicious cycle because they are addicted to their devices.

The brain chemical dopamine plays a role in smartphone addiction. Every time people get a phone notification, their brain releases dopamine. People may receive notifications for texts or "likes" on social media. Dopamine boosts people's mood and makes them happy. *USA Today* columnist Jeff Stibel explained, "Dopamine feels good, so we keep checking our phones, hoping to get a little hit of it."[10] Researchers have found that this process is similar to the high that people get from taking drugs such as cocaine and heroin. People start to use their smartphones more often to get this rush of dopamine. In this way, they can become addicted.

> "Dopamine feels good, so we keep checking our phones, hoping to get a little hit of it."[10]
>
> —USA Today *columnist Jeff Stibel*

Anxiety often arises when people who are addicted to their phones try to ignore them for a long period of time. They may feel disconnected from the world and wonder what they are missing. They may feel distressed if they miss a notification or an alert. They may worry that they are missing out on something important. This feeling is called "fear of missing out," or FOMO. It is very common among smartphone users. For some people, just setting their phones down long enough to have dinner or watch a movie is difficult. They start to feel anxious.

Anxiety and depression can also become issues for people who believe that what they see on social media is an accurate depiction of others' lives. They may begin to feel envious of friends who seem to have more exciting lives than they do. For example, they may feel jealous of people who post a lot of vacation photos on social media. However, the way people portray their lives on social media is often not entirely accurate. Few people chronicle their worst days by posting about them on social media. Instead, they smile, take a selfie, and play up the things that make them look good.

To some people, this envy may seem superficial. But the emotion can be overwhelming for those who experience it. Envy can also be compounded by feelings of isolation. A study published in the *Journal of Abnormal Psychology* in 2019 found that mental health issues, such as depression and suicidal thoughts, had increased significantly among US teens within the last decade. Psychologist

Many people who have smartphones use their phones to take selfies. Some people take and post selfies to boost their self-confidence or get attention.

Jean Twenge, who led the study, thinks that smartphones and social media played a large role in this change. As she explained in an interview with National Public Radio, social media is not as social as its name implies. She said, "You're not having a real time conversation with

someone—usually you're
not seeing their face and
you can't give them a hug;
it's just not as emotionally
fulfilling as seeing someone
in person."[11]

Cutting down on smartphone usage can minimize these negative effects. David Greenfield is the founder of the Center for Internet and Technology Addiction in West Hartford, Connecticut. He recommends that people who are worried about technology addiction do a digital cleanse, during which they refrain from using their smartphones or other devices for an entire day. Although it might not be easy, he told CNBC in 2019, "The first step of the resolution is to prove to yourself that what you're resolving is necessary."[12]

CHAPTER TWO

HOW DO SMARTPHONES AFFECT USERS ON A DAILY BASIS?

The potential long-term effects of smartphone overuse are numerous, but these small gadgets can also have a profound effect on users' daily lives. Smartphone users often rely on their phones throughout the day. They may use their phone's alarm feature to wake up each morning. They may then use the device to check the weather or read the latest news while eating their breakfast. Later, people may use apps while at work. Apps can help them stay organized and do their jobs. They may add upcoming deadlines and appointments for meetings to their smartphone calendars, exchange emails over their phones, and even share documents through apps. Many people

Many smartphone owners use their phones as alarm clocks. They look at their phones right away in the morning when they wake up, often checking social media or other apps before getting out of bed.

use LinkedIn to network professionally, and they may check apps such as Instagram and Facebook during breaks to keep in touch socially. Texting apps such as Messages and WhatsApp make it easy for smartphone users to communicate information in seconds.

While a small fraction of people does not own or use smartphones, an overwhelming majority of Americans—81 percent—own smartphones. Having a

Many people who work from home use both laptops and smartphones to do their jobs. These devices help with different forms of communication.

smartphone is not only desirable but also may be seen as necessary for keeping up with the competition in the professional world. For people who work in sales, for instance, a smartphone is an efficient way to remain available to clients regardless of what kind of communication they prefer. Clients may prefer to text, email, or call. Thanks to smartphones, the salesperson is unlikely to miss the communication.

Smartphones can also make it easier for people who are unemployed to find jobs. Conor Cawly writes for the media company Tech.co. In a 2017 article, he explained: "Whether you're applying for a job, looking up information about a job, or doing online banking . . . [smartphones] have done more than made life easier; they've completely changed the way things get done."[13]

However, there are drawbacks to the ease of communication that comes with smartphones. Smartphone users may feel pressured to be easily reachable and immediately responsive. This is one of the reasons that many users find smartphones to be stressful. Feeling the need to check and recheck a device during off-work

PHANTOM VIBRATION SYNDROME

Many smartphone users experience a strange phenomenon called phantom vibration syndrome. This occurs when people think they feel their phones vibrating even though the devices are neither ringing nor sending alerts. After people place their smartphones in their pockets, they sometimes mistakenly perceive minor movements of clothing or small muscle spasms as phone vibrations. They become convinced that their phones are buzzing when this isn't actually the case.

Robert Rosenberger is an associate professor at the Georgia Institute of Technology's School of Public Policy. As he explained in a 2016 interview with the BBC, many smartphone users have become so accustomed to checking for alerts that they are constantly on edge. Phantom vibration syndrome has become very common. Rosenberger cited a survey of undergraduate students. Ninety percent of the respondents said they had experienced phantom vibrations. These false sensations aren't dangerous, but some smartphone users do find them mildly annoying. Rosenberger thinks researchers need to study the topic more to understand it better.

hours can make employees feel like they are constantly on call. In 2019, Kelsey Gee wrote about job stressors in an article for the *Wall Street Journal*. She explained that a high percentage of working adults feel pressured to be available to their employers via email or work-related apps at all times. She wrote,

> *A recent study by researchers at Virginia Tech, Lehigh University and Colorado State University found that even the expectation of checking work emails on weekends and after-hours triggered anxiety and other harmful effects among workers.*[14]

In response to studies such as this one, some businesses have taken steps to ease the pressure employees might feel to be reachable around the clock. Health care industry management consulting firm Vynamic even created a tool companies can use that prevents messages from bothering employees during their rest or weekend time. The tool, which is called zzzMail, holds off on delivering emails sent after 10:00 p.m. until the next workday at 6:00 a.m. For example, a message sent late on a Friday night will not be received until Monday morning. This allows bosses to send emails whenever it is convenient for them without disturbing their employees' sleep or interrupting their days off.

Approximately 60 percent of cell phone users worldwide use their phones to access the internet. Researchers and other experts think this number will continue to grow.

EFFECTS ON PRODUCTIVITY

Although smartphones have made everyday life easier in many ways, they have also contributed to a decline in productivity due to their addictive qualities. Many people check their phones right away in the morning after they wake up, and their phones are often the last things they look at before going to sleep at night. Some people even spend time on their phones if they wake up in the middle of the night. This can make it difficult for them to feel well rested the next day.

Studies also show that many people are drawn to their smartphones while at work. In a 2017 study by tech analyst company ReportLinker, 60 percent of millennials admitted to using their smartphones to make calls, text, or check social media apps during work hours. Employees might assume that checking their smartphones now and then can't affect their work productivity much, but the truth is that this time adds up quickly. It can also interfere with the focus needed to complete tasks in a timely manner. As *U.S. News & World Report* contributor Robin Madell explained in an article about the problem, "The constant interruption to your work of picking up your phone to check for new messages can, like other workplace distractions, cost you up to six hours a day. This is because task-switching may feel easy to do, but it can take close to twenty-five minutes to resume where you left off."[15]

Experts suggest breaking this habit by setting predetermined times for checking a smartphone at work and not picking it up until then. Setting limits and following through with them can be especially challenging if people need to use their phones to check work messages, but giving coworkers a heads-up can be helpful in this situation. Bosses will likely be pleased that their employees want to focus on being productive and reduce wasted time.

While it is convenient to have resources such as contacts lists and calendars at one's fingertips all the time, the constant access to information that a smartphone provides has had negative effects on the human brain. People no longer have to memorize information such as phone numbers or loved ones' birthdays. When they need to do math, they may use a calculator app on their phones. They also don't have to spend time solving many problems on their own. Internet browsers can help provide solutions and answer users' questions. Studies suggest that a reliance on all these features has turned many people into lazy thinkers. Gordon Pennycook was the coauthor of one study that came to this conclusion. He says, "Our research provides support for an association between heavy smartphone use and lowered intelligence."[16]

PATIENT CARE

In many professions, it is essential that workers pay close attention to their work. Getting distracted while working could have serious consequences. This is especially true for people who work in the medical field. Very few doctors

Some experts call smartphone use by health care providers "distracted doctoring." This practice can result in greater errors when treating patients.

or nurses scroll through their smartphones in the company of patients, but ringtones and text alerts can become distractions during exams or treatments. Phone notifications of any kind can be disruptive. Those disruptive sounds may come from a caregiver's or a patient's device. One study found that just a single interruption by a smartphone during a patient visit increased mistakes in both assessment and treatment by 12 percent.

The stakes are even greater in the operating room (OR), where cell phone use is often not restricted. In some situations, having a smartphone in an OR can improve a patient's care. As *Healthline* writer Cameron Scott wrote in a 2015 article, "Sometimes medical staff outside the operating field consult their phones to look up lab results or potential drug interactions that will help guide medical decisions for the patient."[17] Also, some surgeons use smartphones to look up medical information or to call for assistance when they need another caregiver's help. When seconds count, having this technology readily available could save lives.

However, in other cases, doctors have used cell phones in the OR just to pass the time. Inattention to patients can lead to bad patient outcomes, including death. In a few cases, patients or their families have sued medical professionals such as anesthesiologists who have used cell phones or other digital devices while in the OR. Anesthesiologists give patients medicine that puts them to sleep during surgery. These medical professionals must keep a close eye on their patients' vital signs, such as their heartbeat, throughout an operation. Smartphone distractions can quickly get in the way of this important task. In a 2015 interview with the *Atlantic*, anesthesiologist Peter Papadakos said, "Once we get into or start using our cell phones, we separate ourselves from the reality of where we are. It's self-evident: If you're staring at a phone, you're not staring at the monitors."[18]

Bringing smartphones into ORs can also cause germs to spread in this otherwise sterile environment. In 2015, a group of researchers tested the cell phones of fifty-three surgeons while they were in the OR. Eighty-three percent of those phones contained bacteria. Even after the phones were disinfected, 8 percent of the bacteria remained.

Since smartphones have essentially replaced pagers, most doctors and nurses carry these devices for work purposes. In some medical settings, caregivers also use smartphones, tablets, or laptops to record patient information. While exam tables and other items are wiped down between patients' appointments, these devices may not be cleaned, and they can accumulate bacteria. Some patients end up catching additional illnesses during their stays at hospitals. Researchers are not certain whether bacteria from devices in the patients' rooms are the cause of these illnesses. However, Papadakos and some other experts think this could be the case. The Joint Commission, an organization that develops safety standards for hospitals, recommends that cell phones and other devices be cleaned with disinfectant wipes. Also, a patient's smartphone may pick up bacteria from a hospital or clinic. If the patient does not clean his smartphone, he could become ill from the bacteria.

ACHES AND PAINS

Many news stories have explored how extended smartphone use can lead to eyestrain and bodily aches and pains. Still, many people appear to see these problems as minor compared to the inconvenience of putting their phones down for more than a few hours. Over time, however, these small pains can turn into agonizing afflictions. Researchers have uncovered a link between smartphone usage and migraines. People who tend to get migraines may experience even more of these painful headaches when they overuse smartphones. Moreover, migraine sufferers also appear to be more susceptible to other physical problems after spending too much time on their smartphones. Many migraine sufferers have an extreme sensitivity to light. This condition is called photophobia. After looking at their smartphone screens for long periods of time, these people have a hard time

Children's and teenagers' eyes are more sensitive to blue light than adults' eyes are. Looking at blue light for a long period of time can cause eyestrain, dry eyes, or headaches.

tolerating other types of light. Light that appears normal to most other people seems too bright to them. It can even feel painful.

Too much smartphone use can also lead to pain in other parts of the body. A person's neck and shoulders are the most commonly affected areas. Poor posture can be a considerable factor, as holding a phone for a long period of time in a position that stresses the body, such as bending one's head downward, can trigger pain. Other types of neck and shoulder pain that are linked to smartphone addiction can also trigger headaches. According to spine surgeon Kenneth Hansraj, looking down at 60 degrees places 60 pounds (27 kg) of pressure on the neck. He says, "We recommend that people should continue to enjoy their smart devices, but that they pay specific attention to where their head is in space. You want to be careful that your head is straight up when using a smart device."[19]

Hunching over a smartphone screen for long periods of time can also cause occipital neuralgia. This condition occurs when nerves in the spine become compressed. Although the condition is not life-threatening, the pain it causes is often sudden and severe. Symptoms of occipital neuralgia include pain that moves from the neck or back of the head to the front of the head.

Many of the health problems related to smartphones, including headaches, usually stem from overusing the devices. Dr. Colleen Doherty writes for the website Verywell. She says, "If you find a pattern between high screen time exposure and your migraines, cutting back is a good idea. In fact, you may find that decreasing your screen time . . . improves your overall quality of life and well-being."[20]

HOW DO SMARTPHONES AFFECT THE HEALTH OF SOCIETY?

In 2019, for the first time ever, Americans spent more time on their smartphones than they did watching television. While smartphone use is generally a solitary activity, many people use these devices to text, post to social media, and play games with other smartphone users. This has added an element of peer pressure to owning a phone. Many people, especially young people, may feel like they need to have a smartphone in order to have a social life. Young people who don't have a smartphone may feel pressured to have one if many of their peers have these devices.

Experts estimate that more than 2 billion people around the world have smartphones. Most adults in the United States own a smartphone.

In 2012, 41 percent of US teenagers owned a smartphone. By 2018, this number had skyrocketed to 89 percent. These young smartphone users say their devices provide them with important social connections. A quarter of these teens reported that having access to social media made them feel less lonely.

Still, some parents have resisted giving in to the smartphone craze in favor of wanting their kids to have a more unplugged childhood. They see activities such as playing outdoors, reading, and having in-person conversations to be more valuable than spending time on electronic devices. Sarah Weeldreyer understands the pressure parents face to get smartphones for their kids. In a 2019 article she wrote for the *Atlantic*, she confessed, "My fourteen-year-old son just started high school, and he does not have his own smartphone. When I tell people this, I get the same face I imagine I would if I said that I hadn't fed him for several days."[21]

Of course, not all parents have a negative view of smartphones. Some even consider smartphones to be useful safety tools. Nicole Corning is a working mother who uses her kids' smartphones to track their locations. When she has to work late, an app on her phone tells her what time her kids arrived home from school. The app uses GPS to determine the locations of her kids' smartphones. Corning also uses the app to make sure her kids remain at home until her workday is done. "I need that

GLOBAL SMARTPHONE OWNERSHIP

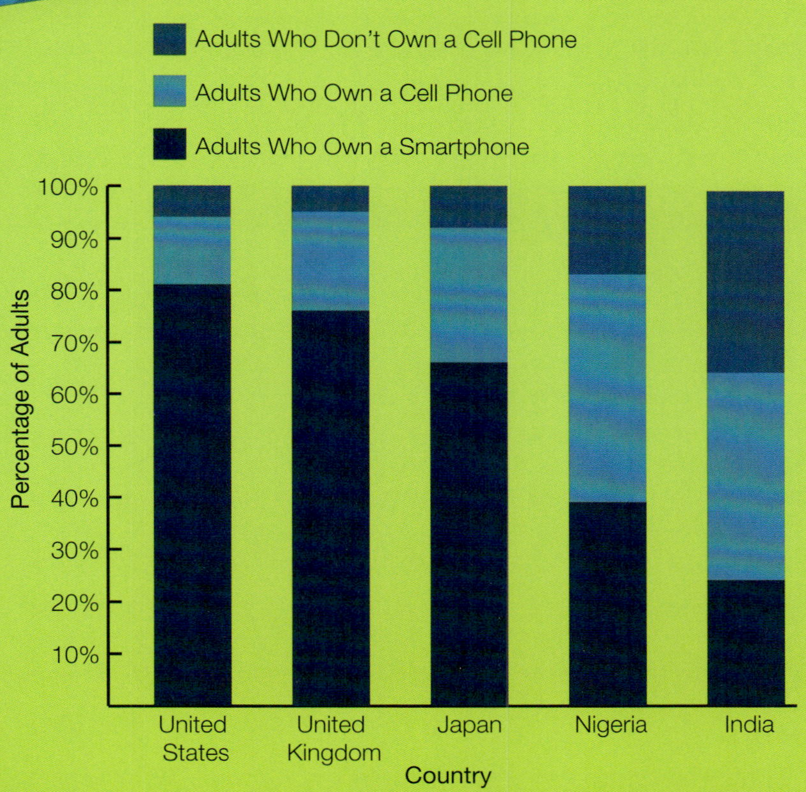

In 2018, researchers surveyed adults in countries around the world about their technology use. Researchers asked respondents whether they owned smartphones or cell phones that are not smartphones. This graph compares smartphone ownership in the United States to smartphone ownership in other countries.

"Smartphone Ownership in Advanced Economies Higher Than in Emerging," Pew Research Center, *February 4, 2019. www.pewresearch.org.*

smartphone as much as my ten and twelve-year-olds think they need it to watch YouTube and Snapchat with their tween friends," she wrote in an article for *Working Mother* magazine in 2017.[22]

MEDICAL ADVICE AND INFORMATION

For all of the negative effects that smartphones can have on people's health, they can also be a practical resource when it comes to both mental and physical well-being. Some people turn to their smartphones when they are not sure whether they need to seek professional medical attention. They may look up their symptoms using a web browser to find out more information about a potential illness or injury. A smartphone can provide fast and reliable information as long as the user only looks at reputable sources. For example, if a child develops a rash after hiking in the woods, a quick web search on a smartphone can help parents identify the cause. They can quickly find articles and photos to help them determine if the culprit was poison ivy, a hairy caterpillar, or another more serious issue that would require a trip to the emergency room (ER).

In the event of a major injury, having a smartphone handy can even save a life. Yonatan Adiri knows this from experience. While she was traveling in China, Yonatan's mother had a serious fall. Yonatan wasn't with her when the

Parents can use health care apps to look up their child's symptoms and find out what may be causing them. Some apps also help users find health care providers in their area.

incident happened, but his father, who had a smartphone, was. Doctors at a local hospital told the Adiris that she had merely broken some ribs. Yonatan's father, however, wanted a second opinion. He snapped photos of his wife's computed tomography (CT) scans. The CT scans were images of her injury. He sent the photos he took to his son, who then showed them to a trauma doctor. The doctor discovered that Yonatan's mother had a punctured lung. As Yonatan told the BBC in 2019, "Who knows what would've happened if he [my father] hadn't taken photos?"[23]

MISDIAGNOSIS

Although smartphones can provide a wealth of useful information, some health websites are inaccurate. People should be careful when using a smartphone or any other internet-enabled device to search for medical advice. Having incorrect information can be just as dangerous as, or even more dangerous than, having no information. Nearly anyone can write a blog or post comments to websites. Articles written by medical professionals are the most reliable sources.

Robyn Carlisle is a nurse. She has seen many patients who have misdiagnosed themselves online. Some have even tried to treat themselves. "Medical information is quickly available with the use of a laptop, tablet, or even a smartphone," she wrote in an article for the *Clinical Advisor* journal. "The key is teaching patients where to look for trustworthy information."[24] She recommends MedLine Plus and the Centers for Disease Control and Prevention (CDC) websites as reliable resources. She also directs her patients to the Medical Library Association website, where they can find a list of other helpful websites and resources.

One of the biggest advantages of smartphones is their speed in leading users to information. While this can be a good thing in an emergency, smartphone users must be careful not to read the information so fast that they misinterpret or overlook important details. When strange symptoms appear, many people want answers quickly. But hasty research—even on reputable websites—can make someone draw the wrong conclusions. People may mistakenly convince themselves they have a serious illness or injury by focusing on only a small part of the picture they gleaned from a quick web search.

GETTING HEALTHIER TOGETHER

Eating right, being physically active, and seeing a doctor regularly are all important parts of a healthy lifestyle. But for many people, the hectic nature of life can get in the way of one or more of these important tasks. Many people regularly consume fast food or unhealthy foods because they are cheap and convenient. These people may not realize how much junk food they eat each day as they rush between home, school or work, and extracurricular activities. Some smartphone apps can help people keep track of their calories and set exercise goals. Health apps can also remind people when it is time to take medications or make an appointment for a routine checkup. Other health apps can monitor users' sleep habits or even check their vision. As of 2019, smartphone users had a choice of more than 300,000 health apps. In 2017, the FDA wrote,

> *Digital health technologies can empower consumers to make better-informed decisions about their own health and provide new options for facilitating prevention, early diagnosis of life-threatening diseases, and management of chronic conditions outside of traditional care settings.*[25]

Peer pressure is often viewed as negative. But in the case of health apps, it has helped shift society's focus toward healthier habits. For example, some popular health apps track the number of steps a smartphone user takes each day. Many encourage the user to take a certain number of steps per day. Smartphone users who are able to improve their health through such tracking apps may spread the word about these apps. Other people, convinced by the apps' success, may start using these apps.

People can also use their smartphones to find a community of like-minded individuals who are interested in getting healthier. Social support is vital for people who want to improve their health. Support from others can help motivate people. Several apps offer a focused form of social media for people looking to lose weight. These people can turn to one another for support on their weight-loss journeys. Some smartphone apps simply offer a virtual meeting place for discussions, while other apps

CALORIE-TRACKING APPS

A study at Stanford University showed that calorie-counting apps can be effective in helping people lose weight. The study followed three groups of people. Researchers instructed people in the first group to keep track of their calories with a calorie-counting app. They told people in the second group to keep track of their weight. Those in the third group did both of these things. All three groups lost weight, but those who both kept track of their weight and used the app lost the most weight and kept the weight off longest. Moreover, the participants who were the most diligent about recording their food intake were the most successful. Of course, people who diet can record their calories without a smartphone, but an app makes the task easier—a benefit that will likely encourage people to keep recording their calories.

connect people to a dietician or nutritionist who serves as a personal coach. Some of these apps have a weekly or monthly cost, but to many people, the support and expert advice they get is worth the investment.

HEALTH SCREENINGS AND MEDICAL CARE

In many ways, smartphones have changed the entire dynamic of visiting a doctor. Before cell phones were invented, one of the only ways to reach a doctor was by calling the doctor's office. A patient would call for an appointment and be seen at the doctor's earliest convenience. If the patient and the doctor had never met, the most the patient would likely know about the doctor was his or her name and specialty. In more urgent situations, patients often ended up seeking treatment in a hospital's ER. In contrast, many patients today have access to smartphone apps that connect them with their doctors' offices. They can use these apps to schedule checkups or sick visits, check their lab results, and read their physicians' bios. In the case of minor emergencies, patients can skip the wait at the ER and instead head to an urgent care provider, which they can also find with the help of a smartphone.

Some health care providers offer telemedicine, which enables a doctor to have a videoconference with a patient

Some health care providers who offer telemedicine use laptops to see and communicate with patients remotely. Telemedicine is helpful for people who live in remote areas or who cannot travel.

through a smartphone or another electronic device. In many cases, this remote exam can be just as effective for diagnosing a new problem or managing an ongoing issue as an in-person visit. During natural disasters or other emergencies in which an in-person visit isn't an option, the ability to conduct an exam this way can be a lifesaving tool. In a 2017 article she wrote for her website, Your GPS Doc, Dr. Nicole Rochester shared, "While these visits were initially used primarily to reach patients in rural areas with poor access to health care, they are now equally popular in urban and suburban settings, where they are used both for convenience and to avoid potentially unnecessary urgent care or Emergency Room visits."[26]

Smartphones have features that can help doctors provide medical care to people in areas of the world that need it the most. Shwetak Patel is an engineering professor at the University of Washington. He says, "If you look at the camera, the flash, the microphone [on a smartphone] . . . they all are getting better. . . . The capabilities on those phones are as great as some of the specialized devices."[27] For example, a smartphone microphone is sensitive enough for a doctor to use it to diagnose asthma. The patient breathes into the microphone. The doctor listens to the patient's breathing to determine if it is normal or labored. A smartphone's camera, when used with the flash, can help a doctor diagnose anemia. Anemia is a condition that occurs when a person's body does not have enough red blood cells to circulate oxygen well throughout the body. A Nexus 5 smartphone has a powerful camera. People who have this phone can take a picture of their finger.

The camera captures light that passes through the finger. Certain changes in color alert the doctor to a deficiency in red blood cells. Patel says, "You can imagine the broader impact of this in developing countries where screening tools like this in the primary care offices are non-existent."[28]

The ability to connect with patients electronically makes many aspects of health care more efficient for everyone involved. People may receive a text from a doctor's office that reminds them of an upcoming appointment or procedure. They may also be able to fill out important paperwork regarding insurance coverage or medical history on their smartphones and submit it electronically ahead of an exam.

Many patients use their smartphones to keep notes about their conditions or to list questions they don't want to forget to ask medical professionals during an appointment. Patients can even use their phones to snap photos of problems such as rashes or swollen joints, which can change dramatically in a short period of time. Patients can bring these photos with them to exams to show how

Pharmacy prescription apps such as FamilyWize and GoodRX help people find affordable medication. The FamilyWize and GoodRX apps are available on Android phones and iPhones.

the problem has progressed. Medical professionals are best equipped to treat patients when they have all the necessary information.

Smartphones can also help people save money on their health care. Medications can be expensive, especially when a patient needs to take a prescription in the long term. Smartphone apps such as GoodRX and FamilyWize can help reduce the cost of prescription medications. The GoodRX app compares the costs of the same prescription from multiple pharmacies, allowing the patient to choose the most affordable option. It also provides coupons that lower prices even further. The FamilyWize app gives users a discount at major pharmacies. Some pharmacies also offer apps that provide customers with discounts or rewards.

While excessive smartphone use has been damaging to society in some ways, two things are also clear: First, the devices are probably here to stay. Smartphones will certainly evolve as technology advances, but they are unlikely to wane much in popularity. Second, when used at proper times and for sensible durations, smartphones can be surprisingly useful tools for the health of the world as a whole.

CHAPTER FOUR

WHAT IS THE FUTURE OF SMARTPHONES AND HEALTH?

As health experts look to the future, many worry about the different ways smartphones may affect people's well-being. Much of this concern stems from the amount of time users spend on their smartphones. This number is rapidly increasing. In 2016, the average person unlocked his or her phone fifty-six times each day. Just two years later, this number jumped to seventy-three times per day. Author Yudhijit Bhattacharjee described this problem in an article for *National Geographic* in 2019. He wrote: "The most compulsive users among us keep our phones within clutching distance at all times, reaching for them even when we wake up in the middle of the night. At airports, on

college campuses, at the mall, at the stoplight—at almost any public place you can think of—the most common sight of our time is that of people with bowed heads, looking intently at their phones."[29]

Some people place the blame on the continual notifications that smartphones deliver. These alerts come from social media apps or other types of apps. Even some games apps send notifications. It is difficult for many people to ignore these alerts. Ethan Kross is a psychologist at the University of Michigan. He explains, "It's well known that if

you want to keep a person dialed into something, give them
a reward at variable times. Turns out, that's exactly what
email or social media does—you don't know when you'll
get another like or receive your next email, and so we keep
checking."[30]

Smartphone users can
silence app notifications in
their settings. They can also
silence their phones while
they do important activities,
such as working, going
to school, or driving. It is
easier for many people to
leave their phones alone if they aren't repeatedly tempted
by notifications.

Many people who spend a lot of time on their
smartphones do not notice the problems smartphone
distractions cause. Splitting their attention between their
real-world activities and those on their smartphones has
become such a habit that they don't even realize they
are doing it much of the time. Psychology professor
Larry Rosen coauthored the book *The Distracted Mind:
Ancient Brains in a High-Tech World*. In an interview
with Bhattacharjee, he explained that smartphones are

distracting people from many important tasks. He says, "It's affecting every aspect of our lives, and sadly, I don't think the pendulum has swung as far as it will go."[31] Rosen thinks people will become even more distracted by smartphones before the situation eventually begins to improve.

GETTING SMARTER ABOUT SMARTPHONE USE

Some people are making an effort to reduce their smartphone usage. Experts recommend that users put addictive apps together in a folder, naming the folder

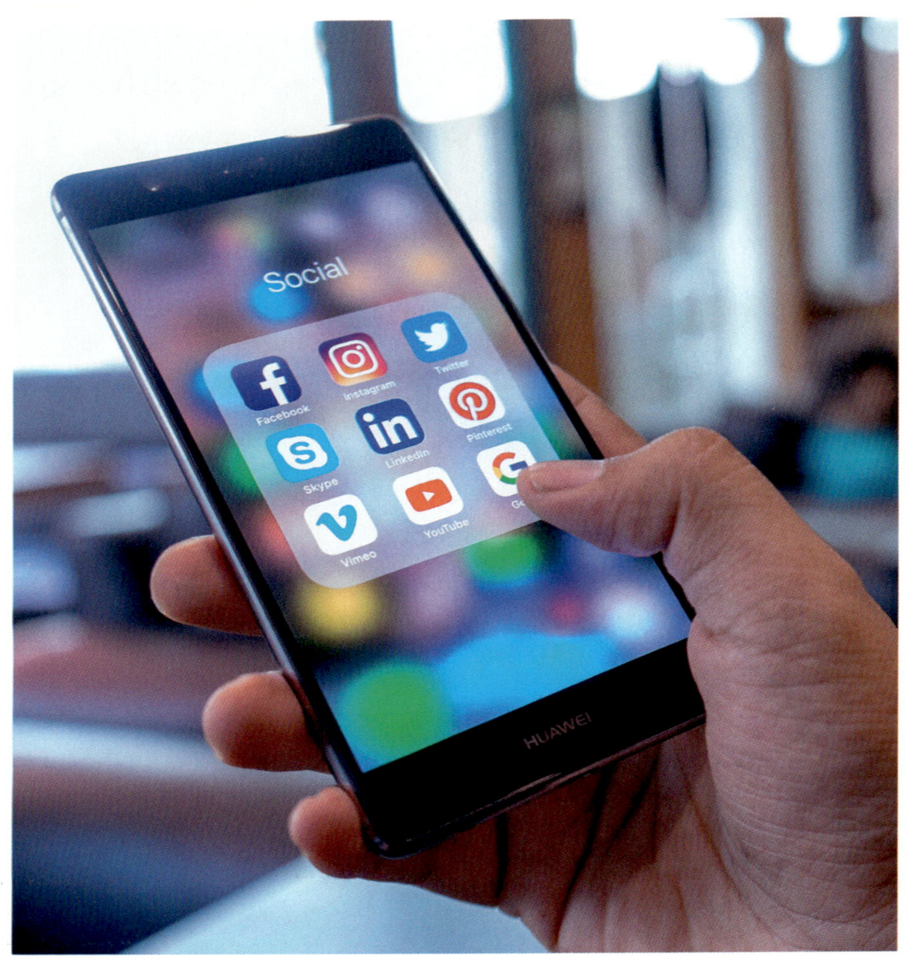

Entertainment apps such as YouTube are among the most popular smartphone apps. Social media apps such as Twitter are also popular.

something that prompts them to think twice before opening it. For example, a user may call the file "Time Wasters." They also recommend that users place this folder on the last page of their phone's home screen. That way, the folder will likely be out of the users' sight and more difficult to access than other apps. Another option is to delete the addictive apps, but some experts think this does not solve the problem. They say that doing so makes it harder for users to stop thinking about the apps and therefore makes it likely that the users will download and become addicted to the apps again.

Surprisingly, even some of the companies that design smartphones are realizing the value of making it easier for users to properly manage their phone time. For example, Apple offers a feature for its iPhones and iPads called Screen Time. Screen Time tracks or limits the amount of time the person spends on the device. Users can turn on Screen Time in their phone settings. They can allow their phones to deliver alerts when a specific time limit has been reached. They can even create time limits for individual apps if they would like to limit the time they spend on certain apps.

EFFECTS ON USERS' MINDS AND BODIES

Researchers are learning more about how smartphone use can affect young people's minds and bodies. Numerous studies are being conducted to find a more concrete link between smartphone overuse and mental health issues in young people. Psychologist Jean Twenge published an extensive study on the subject in 2018. In an article she wrote for the *Atlantic*, Twenge said the generation of people

who were born between 1995 and 2012 are especially
vulnerable to these problems. She calls this generation
iGen because the internet has existed for their entire lives.
She wrote:

> *Rates of teen depression and suicide have
> skyrocketed since 2011. It's not an exaggeration to
> describe iGen as being on the brink of the worst
> mental-health crisis in decades. Much of this
> deterioration can be traced to their phones.*[32]

Research has also shown that heavy smartphone
users may develop physical issues. In addition to painful
conditions affecting people's hands, such as tendinitis
and carpal tunnel syndrome, some scientists think the
human thumb will evolve differently due to the overuse of
smartphones. This could change the way the thumb looks
or even how it works. People are using their thumbs in
different ways than they did in the past. In a 2019 article
on the subject, technology correspondent Rhiannon
Williams wrote: "Young children now are less likely
to hold their hands in a pinch-grip position, and the

rise of touch screens in schooling means their thumbs are used less to grip pens or pencils to write."[33]

Researchers in Australia have even discovered some changes in the human body that are already happening as a result of excessive smartphone use. In 2019, the researchers studied skull X-rays from approximately 400 adults. About a third of the images showed a hornlike growth at the base of the skull, near the neck. This growth is called a bone spur. It is caused by damage that inflammation, or swelling, can cause to cartilage in this part of the body. Normally, this cartilage cushions and protects the joints. However, inflammation can displace the cartilage and prevent it from doing this important job. The surrounding bone responds by growing additional bone. Most bone spurs do not cause problems, but they can cause pain if they rub against other bones or nerves. Health journalist Dr. Shamard Charles reported on this issue for an NBC News article. He noted that bone spurs "often form from repetitive motions. One type of repetitive motion is tilting the head forward, perhaps to look at a smartphone."[34]

DIAGNOSTIC TOOLS AND TREATMENTS

Doctors can already use smartphones to diagnose certain medical conditions. Meanwhile, engineers are working on new apps that could perform even more amazing tasks. Researchers at Stanford University are working on an app that could identify cancerous skin lesions with as much accuracy as an in-person dermatologist. Smartphone users would take photos of their lesions and upload the photos to the app. The app would compare the image with a database of more than 130,000 skin disease images. Researchers at the University of Washington are working on a similar app that could study images of patients' eyes and screen for pancreatic cancer. The app could identify jaundice, or yellowing of the eyes and skin, in the images. Jaundice can be a sign of pancreatic cancer. Dr. Eric Topol is the director and founder of the Scripps Research Translational Institute in La Jolla, California. He says, "The smartphone is becoming the central hub for medicine. Most routine medical tests are about to be smartphone-mediated."[35]

One day, people may even be able to treat conditions such as diabetes with the help of their smartphones. Diabetes is a disease that is caused by a problem with a person's insulin production. Insulin is a hormone made by the pancreas that helps glucose get into the body's cells.

Some people who have diabetes have a glucose sensor on their arm that checks their blood glucose levels. Some sensors can be paired with a smartphone app. The app collects and stores data about the glucose levels.

Glucose is a source of energy that comes from food. In people who are diabetic, their pancreas makes little or no insulin. They need to take doses of insulin. They get this hormone through injections. However, some scientists have

Some smartphone apps are useful for caregivers and their patients. They may store important patient information or help caregivers monitor their patients.

created cells that produce insulin as another potential way to treat people with diabetes. They tested this treatment by injecting the cells under the skin of laboratory mice. They then used a smartphone app to activate the cells' insulin production. They hope to be able to do the same for human patients in the future. The smartphone app would alert users when their glucose levels are too high. The users would then use the app to activate insulin production.

Physical conditions are not the only type of health problems that smartphone technology could address in the future. Researchers at Harvard and Vanderbilt University are also working on ways smartphones can help people who have serious mental illnesses such as depression. For example, doctors could use smartphones to remotely monitor patients who are at a high risk for suicide. This could be done through text messages the doctors and patients exchange at check-in times throughout the day. Special algorithms, or computer processes, would analyze the patients' language. The words people use in conversation can reflect their mental and emotional state. The algorithms could detect concerning patterns, such as language that might indicate suicidal thoughts, that even the human brain may not be able to identify.

THE HEALTH OF THE PLANET

In addition to affecting users' health, smartphones also affect the health of the planet. Pollution comes in many forms, and smartphones have contributed to this problem. In a 2018 article for *Fast Company* magazine, technology writer Mark Wilson said: "Even as the world shifts away from

"Even as the world shifts away from giant . . . PCs [personal computers] toward tiny, energy-sipping phones, the overall environmental impact of technology is only getting worse."[36]

—Technology writer Mark Wilson

giant . . . PCs [personal computers] toward tiny, energy-sipping phones, the overall environmental impact of technology is only getting worse."[36]

Perhaps the most obvious way smartphones are harming the environment is through phone upgrades. Many people regularly upgrade to the newest and most technologically advanced smartphone models. Most users buy a new phone within two years of their previous smartphone purchase. As soon as a new smartphone becomes available for sale, consumers flock to buy it, casting their old smartphones aside without much thought as to what will happen to them. While some companies accept older phones as trade-ins toward new purchases, only a small number of smartphones are typically recycled. For this reason, users who decide to upgrade their phones might consider donating their old phones to a charity such as a women's shelter instead of trading them in for a discount on a new model.

Some users upgrade because their smartphones no longer hold a charge as well as they did in the past. Experts recommend that these users buy a new battery instead of

a completely new phone. This simple step is not only good for the planet, but it will also likely save users a lot of money.

Holding onto a phone for just one more year before trading up can make a big difference in both a user's waste

In 2018, less than 1 percent of smartphones were recycled. Most users do not get rid of their old phones.

production and his or her budget. While smartphones have become abundant in modern society, the materials used to manufacture them are relatively rare. Gold, palladium, platinum, and silver are just a few of the elements found in smartphones. The chips and motherboards made from these items also require a great deal of energy to produce. Other materials inside smartphones can harm the environment when a user throws the phone away. These materials include lead, mercury, and arsenic. They can pollute the land, water, or air when smartphones are buried in landfills or burned in the disposal process.

A little common sense goes a long way in protecting both the planet and people from the potentially damaging effects of smartphones. For example, smartphone users can limit their environmental impact by selecting the best phone models for them at the time of purchase rather than upgrading more often than necessary. Users can also protect themselves from smartphone-related health problems by using the devices in moderation. When used properly, smartphones can make life easier and more enjoyable in many ways. They can even help improve users' health instead of harming it.

SOURCE NOTES

INTRODUCTION: SMARTPHONES AND INJURIES

1. Nellie Bowles, "Me and My Numb Thumb: A Tale of Tech, Texts and Tendons," *New York Times*, May 19, 2018. www.nytimes.com.

2. Quoted in Jacqueline Howard, "Too Much Texting Could Be a Pain in the Wrist, Some Experts Say," *CNN*, June 21, 2017. www.cnn.com.

3. Dan Childs, "7 Surprising Ways Cell Phones Affect Your Health," *ABC News*, March 5, 2009. www.abcnews.go.com.

4. Quoted in Associated Press, "Warning: Reading This on a Smartphone May Cause Anxiety, Researchers Say," *Los Angeles Times*, June 7, 2019. www.latimes.com.

CHAPTER 1: WHAT IS THE LINK BETWEEN HEALTH AND SMARTPHONES?

5. Quoted in Cathy Cassata, "From Selfie Elbow to Texting Thumb: How to Avoid Smartphone Injuries," *Healthline*, March 11, 2019. www.healthline.com.

6. Quoted in Nathan Bomey, "Nearly 6,000 Pedestrians Killed in 2017 Crashes, New Report Says," *USA Today*, February 28, 2018. www.usatoday.com.

7. Quoted in Robert Glatter, "Is Blue Light From Your Smart Phone Harmful to Your Eyes?" *Forbes*, August 31, 2018. www.forbes.com.

8. Quoted in Stephanie Stahl, "Blue Light From Phones, Computers Isn't All Bad, It Can Even Be Therapeutic, Experts Say," *CBS Philly*, May 23, 2019. www.philadelphia.cbslocal.com.

9. Jeff Minerd, "Smartphones Pose Slight Risk to Heart Devices," *Medpage Today*, June 22, 2015. www.medpagetoday.com.

10. Jeff Stibel, "Why You're Addicted to Your Phone . . . and What to Do About It," *USA Today*, July 3, 2017. www.usatoday.com.

11. Quoted in Patti Neighmond, "A Rise in Depression Among Teens and Young Adults Could Be Linked to Social Media Use," *NPR*, March 14, 2019. www.npr.org.

12. Quoted in Jillian D'Onfro, "How to Curb Your Cell Phone Usage This Year," *CNBC*, January 6, 2019. www.cnbc.com.

CHAPTER 2: HOW DO SMARTPHONES AFFECT USERS ON A DAILY BASIS?

13. Conor Cawley, "Don't Kid Yourself: Smartphones Are a Professional Necessity," *Tech.co*, March 9, 2017. www.tech.co.

14. Kelsey Gee, "Sunday Night Is the New Monday Morning, and Workers are Miserable," *Wall Street Journal*, July 7, 2019. www.wsj.com.

15. Robin Madell, "Always Checking Your Smartphone at Work? Here's How to Break the Habit," *U.S. News & World Report*, July 9, 2018. www.money.usnews.com.

16. Quoted in Kendra Cherry, "The Effects of Smartphones on Your Brain," *Verywell*, August 12, 2019. www.verywellmind.com.

17. Cameron Scott, "Do Cell Phones Spread Infections in Hospitals?" *Healthline*, July 22, 2015. www.healthline.com.

18. Quoted in Shefali Luthra, "Texting From the Operating Room," *Atlantic*, July 20, 2015. www.theatlantic.com.

19. Quoted in San Jose Mercury News, "Heads-up: Smartphone Can Cause Neck Strain," *Providence Journal*, December 4, 2014. www.providencejournal.com.

20. Colleen Doherty, "Your Mobile Phone Can Trigger Migraines," *Verywell*, January 9, 2020. www.verywellhealth.com.

SOURCE NOTES
CONTINUED

CHAPTER 3: HOW DO SMARTPHONES AFFECT THE HEALTH OF SOCIETY?

21. Sarah P. Weeldreyer, "I Won't Buy My Teenagers Smartphones," *Atlantic*, September 11, 2019. www.theatlantic.com.

22. Nicole Corning, "The Reasons My Young Children Have Smartphones," *Working Mother*, September 5, 2017. www.workingmother.com.

23. Quoted in Matthew Wall, "'How a Smartphone Saved My Mother's Life,'" *BBC*, February 8, 2019. www.bbc.com.

24. Robyn Carlisle, "The Internet Can't Tell You If You Have Cancer," *Clinical Advisor*, March 11, 2013. www.clinicaladvisor.com.

25. "Digital Health," *U.S. Food & Drug Administration*, December 5, 2019. www.fda.gov.

26. Nicole Rochester, "5 Ways to Use Your Smartphone to Improve Doctor Visits," *Your GPS Doc*, September 3, 2017. www.yourgpsdoc.com.

27. Quoted in Jean-Louis Santini, "Smartphones Are Revolutionizing Medicine," *Phys.org*, February 18, 2017. www.phys.org.

28. Quoted in Jean-Louis Santini, "Smartphones Are Revolutionizing Medicine."

CHAPTER 4: WHAT IS THE FUTURE OF SMARTPHONES AND HEALTH?

29. Yudhijit Bhattacharjee, "Smartphones Revolutionize Our Lives, But at What Cost?" *National Geographic*, January 25, 2019. www.nationalgeographic.com.

30. Quoted in Yudhijit Bhattacharjee, "Smartphones Revolutionize Our Lives, But at What Cost?"

31. Quoted in Yudhijit Bhattacharjee, "Smartphones Revolutionize Our Lives, But at What Cost?"

32. Jean M. Twenge, "Have Smartphones Destroyed a Generation?" *Atlantic*, September 2017. www.theatlantic.com.

33. Rhiannon Williams, "Our Smartphone Obsession Could Affect How Future Humans' Hands Evolve," *iNews*, June 14, 2019. www.inews.co.uk.

34. Shamard Charles, "Tech Disorder? Smartphones Linked to Bizarre Horn-Like Skull Bumps," *NBC News*, June 20, 2019. www.nbcnews.com.

35. Quoted in Dennis Wise, "Smartphones Are Changing Medical Care in Some Surprising Ways," *NBC News*, October 13, 2017. www.nbcnews.com.

36. Mark Wilson, "Smartphones Are Killing the Planet Faster Than Anyone Expected," *Fast Company*, March 27, 2018. www.fastcompany.com.

FOR FURTHER RESEARCH

BOOKS

Judy Dodge Cummings, *Apple*. Minneapolis, MN: Abdo Publishing, 2019.

Harry Henderson, *How Mobile Devices Are Changing Society*. San Diego, CA: ReferencePoint, 2016.

Susan Henneberg, *Are Mobile Devices Harmful?* San Diego, CA: ReferencePoint, 2017.

Patricia D. Netzley, *How Do Cell Phones Affect Health?* San Diego, CA: ReferencePoint, 2015.

Bradley Steffens, *Cell Phone Addiction*. San Diego, CA: ReferencePoint, 2020.

INTERNET SOURCES

"8 Smart Uses for Your Smartphone," *Northwestern Medicine*, 2019. www.nm.org.

Wendy L. Patrick, "How Your Smartphone Can Make You Healthy and Happy," *Psychology Today*, August 5, 2018. www.psychologytoday.com.

Jean M. Twenge, "Stop Debating Whether Too Much Smartphone Time Can Hurt Teens, and Start Protecting Them," *Time*, March 21, 2019. www.time.com.

WEBSITES

HelpGuide
www.helpguide.org

HelpGuide is a nonprofit organization focused on mental health and wellness. Its mission is to educate and empower people by providing free information about mental health issues. It offers information about smartphone addiction and the related health effects on its website.

National Highway Traffic Safety Administration
www.nhtsa.gov

The National Highway Traffic Safety Administration strives to keep people safe on US roadways. Its work helps reduce deaths and injuries from motor vehicle crashes. It provides information and statistics about distracted driving.

Psychology Today
www.psychologytoday.com

On this website, psychologists and other experts offer information and advice on mental health and related issues. Researchers explore the effects behaviors and activities, such as smartphone use, can have on people's health.

INDEX

IMAGE CREDITS

Cover: © fizkes/Shutterstock Images
5: © Image Point Fr/Shutterstock Images
6: © mady70/Shutterstock Images
8: © Kinga/Shutterstock Images
11: © mimagephotography/Shutterstock Images
12: © Oleksii Didok/Shutterstock Images
22: © goodluz/Shutterstock Images
25: © Stockshakir/Shutterstock Images
26: © Dean Drobot/Shutterstock Images
29: © Iakov Filimonov/Shutterstock Images
32: © Michael Jung/Shutterstock Images
36: © Peter Snaterse/Shutterstock Images
39: © Page Light Studios/Shutterstock Images
41: © Red Line Editorial
43: © Aleksandra Suzi/Shutterstock Images
49: © Agenturfotografin/Shutterstock Images
52: © Dragana Gordic/Shutterstock Images
55: © Monkey Business Images/Shutterstock Images
58: © Nopparat Khokthong/Shutterstock Images
63: © Andrey Popov/Shutterstock Images
64: © Reshetnikov_art/Shutterstock Images
67: © Dmytro Balkhovitin/Shutterstock Images
68: © Parilov/Shutterstock Images

ABOUT THE AUTHOR

Tammy Gagne has written dozens of books for both adults and children. Her recent titles include *Women in the Workplace* and *Dealing with Self-Injury Disorder*. She lives in northern New England with her husband, son, and a menagerie of pets.